John Metcalf
Sept. 88

Hiram and Jenny

Hiram and Jenny

RICHARD OUTRAM

The Porcupine's Quill, Inc.

Art is by Barbara Howard.

Published by The Porcupine's Quill, Inc., 68 Main Street, Erin, Ontario N0B 1T0 with the financial assistance of the Canada Council and the Ontario Arts Council.

Distributed by The University of Toronto Press, 5201 Dufferin Street, Downsview, Ontario M3H 5T8.

Printed and bound in April, 1988 by The Porcupine's Quill. The stock is Zephyr laid, and the type, Cartier.

ISBN 0-88984-118-7

This book is for Barbara.

Hiram with Banjo

The broken-off telephone pole
by the shack by the ramshackle sea
points nowhere. The tilted sky is green.
He grins. He admires to see

blue smoke from the three-legged stove
torn over the lion dunes
and swirled in the serpent grass.
He plucks at old crimson tunes,

and spits with the wind. Black rocks beat back
ragged remembering waves.
He is going to have him another drink.
Or two. Well, Jesus saves.

Hiram and Jenny

Banjo, by-and-by.
Woman, everywhere
out in the basswood night
and Jenny is there.

Is in the next empty cabin
in the next room is near
musk now snake-naked
yes Jenny is here.

And bucks plunge from the sun
and trouts leap from the sea
and fall back and waves waves
break Jenny and me.

Morning is scrawny, scorched
where the dog-star shone.
Hiram I lay me down to die.
Jenny is gone.

Creek

Rises, mother cold
from a rusty old
bottomless washtub
up in the spruce scrub,
flows as water will
intricately downhill,
lets, as water may,
nothing block its way,
writhes and twists and bends
back but still descends
to clefts where, lying flat
on his belly, hat
jammed over his eyes,
silent Hiram lies,
reaching deeply, slow,
fondling the flow,
deft to tickle out
a living ingot trout
for Hiram's black fry pan,
and cuts as water can,
around a boulder's flank,
a hollow in the bank,
lined with shards of shale,
where Hiram keeps his pail
and bent tin dipper hid,
since someone stole the lid,
then quickens past the back
of Hiram's slanted shack
a sudden silver thrust
and as sweet water must
dashes down to be
salted with the sea.

Down at the Station

Finest crop of burdock in three counties.
Chunks of amethyst glass, from the telegraph poles,
picked off with a 22. No stove-pipe left.
Platform sagged like old swampboards, full of holes.

So nobody goes nowhere any longer.
Nothing gets shipped out and nobody comes.
Nobody hangs around under the slat awning:
no dogs, no drummers, no railroad dicks, no bums.

Windows broken and boarded, doors smashed open.
They took the last of the rails, just after the war.
To make razor blades out of, somebody said.
No endless silver ribbon to wind up any more.

So all of the folk hereabouts, they like it,
are still where they always have been. Men forget.
Hiram, borrowing shingles, saw him by torchlight,
stomping. He will be slain some night. But not yet.

Off the Hook

Semblance of beasts in the trees.
Dulled nuggets along the ground.
He glares at the cobalt sky.
With a single imperfect bound,

the blood-flecked buck has leapt
the intricate river. He
is mortal. And twinned suns
quench in the hammered sea.

Gobbets of cinnabar green,
alizarin reds, and black
made from burnt ivory.
The cerulean roof is slack.

It is time to begin; the wind,
fallen, has seen to that.
The Immortals have doffed their plumes.
Hiram puts on his hat.

Helios

Gets her up like a ball of string
burning, a mess of firesnarls,
summers, from out of the white swampfire
back of the black alders.

Winters, a fried duck egg on its side,
pulled out of the green sea. Tell me,
water won't burn.

Mornings, Miss Alice sets soaking her up
on her back stoop, until the rheumatics
lets her get out to the privy on her own.
Bone-stubborn.

Dead of noon, I says to my shadow,
'Wobble, Boy, wobble. But don't you go
leaving old Grailey all alone by hisself.
Not just yet.'

Afternoons, can burn you your bare hand
on the flivver doorhandle. Makes
that tar snake dance. Right into town.
Body can't glare back;

but evenings, sometimes, we both settles down
to stare out each other, eyeball to eyeball,
like tomcats fixing to spat.
Sees who blinks first. Mostly, I do.

Hell, there's no man in the hammered moon,
see for yourself, most dead nights.
But sun is.

Secrets

1   Thinking on going into town,
pick up the Government check,
and some Dr. Earle's blue embrocation
for the miseries in his neck.

Unless it comes pissing down.
Then Hiram will set in his shack,
rocking, and watching the pock-marked ocean
leaving and coming back

As it always does, but once,
when the southern sun stood still
and the waves warped and the waters parted.
Hiram caught him a chill.

2   Old Earle has a speciality oil
he mixes in with his dough;
stinks to high heaven, like Earle.
Sure catches mudcat though.

You peels the skin off like a glove;
one slit up the belly, to pluck
out the whole snarl of innards.
Pop the swim-bladder for luck.

Aunt Ruby said she could say,
by the look of a mess of guts,
was some body going to die.
And they said, she was nuts.

Hiram Beachcombing

Never know what comes ashore
after a three-day blow.
Once picked me up the soused *Works*
of Edgar Allan Poe,

just fine for lighting the stove.
Another time, I found
all was left of a ship's log;
said, she had run aground,

on the last page, breaking up fast.
Ended her with a prayer,
or a old text, to Merciful God
for the Souls on board her there.

Another time was a bottle
with a message inside that said
things I wished it didn't.
Gone right out of my head.

Came across a pine coffin.
On the inside of one plank
someone had scratched a cross.
The outside side was blank.

Find me a lot of speechifying,
poems, journals, love-letters, and such.
Once a Testament writ in blood.
Don't do, to read too much.

Fire Hall

Number One Pumper, suck up the whole ocean,
leave all the cods popeyed,
fill Tuggle's Valley in a half-hour!

Number Two Ladder, reach to the moon
and piss on it,
or the top of Steadman's pink neon sign!

Red-hot-pokers across the front, geraniums,
lawn like a matelot's haircut, play pool on it,
paints the stones white once a week.

Fyles's kid, Jonathan, shinnied up the hose tower,
fell and bust his left arm. Big to-do.
Because it was there.

Best checker team anywheres, in the back.
Big Morrie did every crossword in The Clarion
for eleven years straight, never misses.

Got them a black-and-white coach dog,
name of Turner, but real friendly,
sleeps in the cab, mornings.

Late red nights, by himself,
Hiram slides up and down
the polished brass pole.

Palace

Tuesday nights, they hand you out your free dishes,
Thursdays, tea-towels. Anyways, Hiram don't pay,
not when it's Jenny is taking in the tickets,
which it is at the Saturday afternoon matinee.

That Big Bertha, shoots her shells right over
the English Channel, the one some fat girl swum,
slathered herself in beargrease, wore bug-goggles.
Jap battleship blown to Kingdom Come.

Kiss more horses than girls, but they're not pansy,
in the serial. Hopalong always wears white,
all of the bad hombres sashay around the homestead,
get blind drunk, shoot up everything in sight.

Never did much care for the Three Stooges,
brothers slapping brothers, or one would goose
the other, real mean streak. Like the Gladson boys,
everyone says that they all got two screws loose.

Feature, Bette Davis gets herself into big trouble,
seems like she's wild for this young English Duke,
talks like he burned his lip on a hot fritter,
But his momma don't like Americans. Make you puke.

Jenny stands at the back to see the Bugs Bunny,
poor old Elmer Fudd, Bugs drives him mad,
ends up gnashing on carrots. Funny thing is,
most of the other cartoons leaves you sad.

And everybody is champing, shifting, restless,
like the beasts tethered down in the hold of the Ark.
In by noon, out blinking, suppertime. Peace:
for all colours, mind, will agree in the dark.

Flight

Once, at the Fall Fair,
five dollars-fifty
Hiram got to soar

for near ten minutes.
Slicker-yellow biplane
with only Hiram in it

behind the goggled ace,
who chewed cut plug.
Height didn't faze

Hiram, all in all,
didn't like the racket,
the hot-oil smell.

Saw his own speck shack,
the bended blazed sea,
the flat world intact.

Always said he'd do it:
landed without him,
pilot never knew it,

Hiram off on his own
in the tunneled sun
in the white swoon down.

Skein

October morning, Jenny
headed for Steadman's, purchase
a dress pattern; stopped cold.

Geese come over low, fast,
just took off from Gaunt's marsh
where there's still wild rice,
making one hell of a racket;
lopsided vee, maybe fifty
or more, the leader out front
reaching, a few stragglers,
forming and reforming, rising,
headed back south. Powerful.

Watched them until they became
slight wavering smoke, then
lost into high light suffered
the bright dread remembered
battering inwards until
two crows beat back, black,
into the wind, ragged, raucous,
recalled her to hereabouts.

Had she survived, just might
have christened her Helen;
well, can't name a girl child
Pollux. Helen will pass.

Techne

Hiram is washing his socks in the creek.
Not far offshore, unseen,
crammed with warheads and comic books,
a nuclear submarine

noses about with her cornfed crew,
bored, but ready to cope
at the drop of a ciphered word. Alas,
Hiram has lost the soap,

which, being Sunlight, not ninety-nine
and forty-four hundredths percent
pure, sinks. Some folks' troubles
is trying to pay the rent,

others, it's what her dad will say
when he finds out she's three months gone.
The sub, summoned, buggers off.
Hiram puts back on

his socks and paddles his feet awhile,
best way to rinse them out.
One is yellow and one is green,
with orange stripes. No doubt,

God's socks match in mysterious ways.
Washed in the Blood of the Lamb,
the Dead shall rise up on the Last Day.
Hiram don't give a damn.

Cynic

Jenny admires snakes.
Lives simple, but got style.
knows an adder who occupies
a broken weeping tile.

Jenny encountered him
once, sloughing his skin;
asked, could she help extricate,
they being sort of kin?

Serpent said thanks but no,
sloughing a job for one;
best thing, could she step aside,
stop blocking the sun.

Jenny, occasions, thinks
being Jenny is no great shakes:
but wouldn't be adder however much
Jenny admires snakes.

Age

It is how things goes missing, most troubles Grailey.
Nothing much you can do about, though.
Not like the hatchet, walked right out of the wood-shed;
Grailey figures he knows just where that would go,

Ephraim Silk was always a touch light-fingered,
get it back, with one of Silk's shoats, some night.
Our losses, Pastor Gwyllym call Acts of God.
Well some, maybe; others is men's all right.

But Grailey can't picture rightly his grand-daddy's smile;
spread slow, sidelong, one side, after his stroke,
curl round his pipestem, reach to pucker his eyes,
kindly, watch Grailey delighting, through the smoke.

And more and more nowadays Grailey disremembers
his granny's cradle conjure, truth she could part see,
Godbody cautions, spells, consolation, flame witness,
the rare terrible names of things bright to be.

Sunday

Never did throw stones at birds.
But Jenny and Hiram walk about,
make it different from other days
by night. More loving, more devout.

Hiram and Ludwig

Turned up, sat in the shack
one night. Was pretty deaf,
muttered on about the sea,
it being the bass clef.

Come to hear him some banjo,
so I picked, he hummed along,
bit off-key, but not too bad.
Moon like a kicked gong

come thrumming through the doorway.
Now that, the man could hear;
most folks, moon goes in one,
right out the other ear,

don't know them where to harken.
Had some whisky, anyway,
asked him about the Afterlife;
said, 'Hiram, can't rightly say.',

more or less, in German,
but seems I could comprehend;
said, 'Trick is, times, to mosey,
she sorts out in the end.'

Said, 'Things is good, is strictly
banjo, is by consent.'
Stared a while at the coal-oil lamp,
smiled, and up and went.

Feely

Feely's mother had ten kids,
    lost her five,
pretty tough, depression times,
    keep them alive.

Feely the titman of the lot,
    wasn't bright,
bit of a hare lip, one pink eye,
    not quite right.

Didn't last too long at school,
    got the strap
near every day, for losing fights.
    Couldn't scrap.

Real given names was Alonzo Thomas
    Archibald,
well, small wonder Feely's all
    he's ever called.

Never wore but his brothers' old
    hand-down clothes.
Body can't tell what Feely's thinking,
    what he knows;

Claims he once saw Jesus Christ
    on Tuggle's pond
walk across the water lugging
    a palm frond,

folks don't pay much heed. Feely
    talks a lot,
to himself, mostly. Hell, you takes
    what you got.

but now and again he and Hiram
    gets to fool
around together, coon-whicker nights,
    and banjo duel.

Kite in Sun

Something living up there struggling,
like fishing in the air,
darkness visible has hooked on Hiram
good, but he don't care

to leave the ground yet, maybe later,
for now, too much to cleave.
Not the first high wildness threaten
Hiram here, and leave

him standing holding a conundrum
in his grasp: a mortal sin,
let slip this bright blindness upwards,
or wind it in.

Trample

Orange flame out front of Hiram's shack,
daylilies, three great sprawling wedges,
kind of a tan-amber-orange, petals dark,
like rashers of crisp bacon, at the edges.

They thrive right out in the full noon sun,
wicked, would turn a strong man's head.
Some of them reach as tall as Hiram's momma,
she had a fancy for them. But she's dead.

She never set them out, been there it seems
forever and a day. Getting a bit of a mess,
roots choked up, need of dividing, Jenny says.
Well some off-days, so is Hiram I guess.

Sits alone on his porch, soulful evenings,
watching them fade. Don't last the night,
being by nature but daylilies. They are
all gone into the world of light!

Tarr

Hiram's old cat, Tarr, is well nigh blind.
Eyes gone both smoke-opal now. Pure white,
with black socks, from walking on hot asphalt,
Jenny says. Can still see light.

Was in her time a most famous mouser.
Plenty of them about, she used to bring
one in mornings, to drop on Hiram's pillow,
tail like a bit length of wet brown string,

then wash, pleased with herself. Hiram figures
he could have come to thrive on fried-mouse stew.
Didn't fetch her, she just turned up, remarking,
took over the whole place the way cats do.

Hiram figures she could walk on water,
had a mind to, never leave a mark,
way she steps cat-fashion, greatly admires
manner white cats can vanish in the dark.

Sleeps all day, like someone dropped her there.
Lord only knows, how many piebald litters
she raised up in her day, or how much Hell.
Lets you get too fond, times, of His critters,

knows best perhaps. Her bright circle
is banked fires, is white light's cache,
can see right through her when she stretches,
is become sun, mostly, and fine white ash.

Ferry

Hiram ponders on taking the ferry,
leaves from Karen's wharf, most every evening;
go live in Halifax, Montreal, Toronto,
had him lots of friends there already,
made the move over the years.

Thought of nothing else, for a time,
a while back, things was bad, getting
harder and harder, keep body and soul
together. But thought the better of it,
finally. And Jenny dead set against it.

Wasn't that he couldn't raise the fare,
could sell up the shack, move out.
Wouldn't get much for her, considering,
but enough. Still lots of folks like living
here, town's not quite out in the sticks.

Thing is, once you leave, most mortal souls,
they never gets back. Not ever.

Ark

Been raining steady, what seems like forty days,
settled after the blow into a straight drizzle,
whole world drenched, wetter, as Hiram says,
than a bull's pizzle.

Not that Hiram cares, mind you, he likes the rain,
launching his shack at last. He sleeps a lot,
drifted across the featureless waters' face
in his iron cot,

keeper, most of his night, of the paired beasts,
restive deep in the hold, loose-penned on the deck,
nipping or nuzzling Hiram. For better or worse,
it's Hiram's neck;

man who minds, he takes it upon himself
his beasts' burden; likewise his creatures keep
Hiram, wherever his blest kind be, human throughout
his mortal sleep,

that, as together they rest, together they waken
to go forth, replenish, multiply one by one,
God willing, anew under the first-burning
Dove-ravening sun!

Adjuration

Look to the pismire, Hiram,
   you slug-a-bed!
Emmets, not lambs, number,
   you sleepy-head!

Time is a-wasting, Hiram,
   work to be done,
ants set you to hustle
   under the sun!

All man's estate to harvest,
   before night falls!
Hiram yawns, rolls over,
   mutters 'Balls!'

Hiram's Ladder

Ladders come two sizes,
too short, too long.
Hiram's had his ages,
got it for a song.

Gone all grey and splintery,
left out in the rain,
rungs is worn and puckered
along the grain.

Ladder is might handy,
a body has to cope,
use it, dry your washing,
use it to elope,

use it, cross on thin ice,
get you into town,
use it, let God's Angels
mosey up and down.

His does Hiram, gets him
where he wants to be;
borrow the odd apple
from Manson's Pippin tree,

get up to the shack roof,
caulk the stove-pipe ring,
clear the bottom of the well,
can reach to anything

Hiram needs. But neighbour's kid
borrowed it, young Gaunt,
left it leaning on the moon.
'I want! I want!'

32

Given Pause

Like light broken.
But are no words.
Ever. Woodsmoke froze.
Stopped up the birds.

And Hiram sees Hiram
riven plain as day
resplendent O Hiram!
Like the man say,

in my father's house,
plenty of rooms.
Meantime Hiram.
Heretofore resumes.

On his momma's side,
even sticks and stones,
sometimes. Hiram
knows in his bones.

Grace

Thirties was depression,
but momma made do.
Cooked up fish-head soup,
root-vegetable stew,

had an awful lot of beans,
fatback was a treat
saved for Sundays, never
nothing left to eat,

Beehive corn syrup,
wood tub of sauerkraut,
got the neck and Pope's nose,
or the Parson's snout,

always was an iron pot,
back of the stove,
everything went into it.
With momma's love,

she knew bread is broken,
water truly wine,
vittles is His body.
Got along just fine.

Settled with a mug of tea,
a plate of fried scrods
and onions, Hiram
looks up, nods.

Hangover

Jubilant, triumphant,
has too much to say,
Hiram's head considered,
about the break of day.

Black weather-vane profile
against the first light,
up on the pump handle;
always gets it right,

but goes over it again,
as if reproving men's
frailties and follies,
not to mention hens',

as if mad master rooster
had hatched the bloody sun;
which, maybe, Hiram figures,
he did, this one.

'... rare original heartsblood'

Was old throb-throat, as Hiram used to name him;
gold-slitted pair of top-mounted knobkerrie eyes;
been hanging around in the garden, ages and ages;
liked bugs and slugs, but also inclined to flies.

One thing about him, knew how to wait forever,
sit squat all morning under a mullein leaf,
then lunge sudden, tongue-flick too quick to see,
and another amber dragonfly come to grief.

A warted beauty, his gnarled, swart-spotted back
ridged like the backs of Hiram's granny's hands,
that dandled him once. Wrinkled, pale-cream-leather
Buddha belly; well, is Buddha, Hiram understands,

or was. Coon got him, gutted him out last night,
what's left shrivelled, curled like a cast-off glove,
flies frantic about his gaped, eyeless, astonished face
that only God, or a grandmother maybe, could love.

Rabbit

All kinds of rabbits
den up in Silk's wood lot,
some is only cottontails,
some is not,

some is randy buck jacks,
they can run like stink,
can sit there being furred stones,
not even blink;

some, like Hiram's momma says,
gets ants in their pants,
meet up with Hiram, moonlight nights,
mad to dance.

Brothers

Not natural to man, in Anse's judgement;
go down winter mornings before first light,
come up, shift finished, into bitter darkness,
work all day in a staggered, lamp-pocked night.

Fresh ponies, old times, they went down but once,
got back up once, straight to the knacker's yard.
Folks figured the boys to be dead lucky,
no money about, jobs scarce, the times were hard.

Spent two years steady, driller, up at the coalface,
worked bent over beastwise, ten hours a crack;
then Anse was killed, was crushed by a wild trolley.
Hiram came up that noon and never went back.

Remembers sometimes, stretched out gazing seawards,
eyes tight-squinted against the huge white glare
bounced back fierce from the everburning water.
Occurs to Hiram, how Anse is still down there.

They would cough, hawk, spit black all day, Sundays,
The Lord's Day, Sunday, that is the day of rest.
'... Sabbaoth God, graunt me that Sabaoths sight.'
Radix omnium malorum cupiditas est.

Metaphysic

1   The horizon line is heat-hazed:
that just might be a sail,
or an undiscovered continent.
The best conjectures fail

for lack of validation.
Hiram saw the sun
set the other morning,
didn't tell anyone,

things being, at rock-bottom,
elegantly askew.
Truth is the cry of all, but
the game of the few.

2   Hiram figures Hiram to be
    a freak in fact,
    there being only but one Hiram,
    caught in the act.

    One Hiram is plenty,
    the skewed truth be told;
    Hiram the clouted infant,
    Hiram here growing old,

    Hiram who sired the sun
    before the first Word was said,
    Hiram's Hirams ranged between
    Hiram unborn and dead

    are Hiram everpresent.
    Jenny gives a sigh,
    sleepy, shifts slightly
    one troutwet thigh.

The Night it Rained Cats and Dogs

The night it rained cats and dogs,
Hiram was prepared, Jenny was standing by,
had a bucket under the drip by the stove,
a copper washtub at the ready;
but they weren't much help, in fact,
as things worked out.

The first to come down was a grizzled old Chow,
lit with a scrabble of claws on the lino,
took off into the night, mauve tongue lolling.

Then a Manx tabby, rather great with child;
Hiram's old Tarr had rude things to say
about her tail and her morals, both,
but the mother-to-be took into consideration
Tarr's great age and position and let it pass.

Next, a particularly nasty tangle of squash-faced Peke
with smelly breath, nobody's favourite,
and a pair of virulent, yapping Yorkies;
somebody up there glad to get rid of them,
was Jenny's guess.

Then, a Persian Blue tom, landed perfectly, delicate
on all fours, of course, and started right in
to wash very thoroughly one immaculate paw.

Things got a bit hectic round about midnight,
when an entire team of sled-dogs, Siberian Huskies
with strange pale arctic-lit distant eyes
plummeted, still in their traces, hungry,
and Hiram was short of frozen char.

One calico matron, flustered by the turn of events,
slashed Hiram on the ankle, unexpected,
and a surly young Doberman named Gerhardt
nipped Jenny's bottom. Didn't break the skin.
Won't try that again soon, for sure.

And on and on. Hiram thought maybe, later,
that he recognized one brindled lurcher,
used to belong to old man Silk, years back,
but lit out hell-for-leather one day
and who could blame him? All of the cats
being an unknown quantity, but of high quality.

There were a few spats; one high-toned Saluki
took exception to being used as a landing pad
by an elegant little seal-point Siamese, Jenny
sorted that out right off. And once Hiram
had to lay down the law to a Bull Terrier bitch,
Magnolia, who figured the shack, for that matter
the world, was no place for cats of any complexion.
But all in all they carried on pretty tractable
for a downpour of mixed creatures.

Hiram kept a rough count, off the record:
it came to thirty-two dogs, eleven bitches,
and about one hundred and sixty-three cats,
mostly of indeterminate gender. Not too bad,
all things being considered, for beginners.

And long about daybreak, one Catamount descended:
vouchsafed in flamed error, maybe, for who can account?
Everyone froze. But she bounded, flanks blazing,
out, trailing a tangle of dangerous sparks,
leaving darkness swirling behind her awhile.

By morning, it had let up, Hiram and Jenny
were bushed, went back to bed, silenced
by various dazed animal eyes, beasts kindled
or rekindled into our feral time.

Grief

Jenny lost her baby.
It was a small loss, and went almost unnoticed.

Some people were kind and some were not.

Now she can no longer walk past certain boulders
or look at peonies.

And sometimes, continuing along the shore, she seems
to hesitate, as if about to turn back.

Most evenings and first thing mornings.

Her eyes, which were dark, have darkened.

Hiram went out and split five cords
of maple in three days.

Sometimes exhaustion helps, a little.

Grief Tree

And shortly thereafter, Hiram and Jenny
went out together and planted a Rowan berry tree
on a bare slope behind the shack.

Because the planting of Rowan is a meet act.
Because the fruit of Rowan is orange-vermilion,
    the colour of some fire.
Because the toothed leaves of Rowan are spread canopy.
Because Rowan provides perch for occasional birds
    who sing from it uttermost song.
Because Rowan is life which endures.
Because Rowan is death.
Because the reach of Rowan is Rowan.
Because Rowan is of Rowan and begets Rowan.
Because the shaft of Rowan is Jesse's rod.
Because Rowan uplifted is Yggdrasil.
Because to look on Rowan restores the weary who are heartsick.
Because Rowan points to the azure firmament.
Because Rowan entertains the least wind and trembles thus.
Because Rowan by day stands between the sun.
Because Rowan by night indicates the wheeling constellations,
    which are various figures.
Because Rowan is passion.
Because Rowan is emblem which is beloved.
Because this world will not be deprived of Rowan.
Because Rowan speaks to Rowan, with no name.
Because God has looked on Rowan especial.
Because Rowan is the right shape, being a broad taper.
Because Rowan shall perish being Rowan and shall not perish.
Because the daughters of men are Rowan,
    the sons and the daughters of men.

Because Rowan makes slight sound in the wind.
Because Rowan is for all seasons.
Because Rowan in summer is bounteous dark seagreen.
Because Rowan in winter is spare calligraph.
Because Rowan in springtime bears clusters of cream blossom,
    which summon the honeybee.
Because Rowan in autumn lets fall its leaves
    but keeps its scarlet fruit which are wounds.
Because Rowan is consolation and there is none.
Because Rowan drinks in the light, which is of the sun.
Because Rowan is silver-greaved in moonlight.
Because the animal bark of Rowan is cool to the cheek.
Because Rowan is creature and we are Rowan.
Because Rowan casts small shadow at noonday
    and long shadow morning and evening.
Because Rowan has chinks of light and the bark is dappled.
Because Rowan is lamentation and rejoicing.
Because Rowan does not let up but remains.
Because the roots of Rowan reach down to rock
    to encircle the earth.
Because Rowan transpires water, which falls from above.
Because Rowan enters the air.
Because Rowan bears fire.
Because Hiram and Jenny shall see it hereafter and know Rowan.
Because in Rowan all manner of thing shall be well.

Hiram's Rope

Hiram has a curious length of rope;
seems, somehow, to have a life of its own,
find it lying about in the strangest places,
never quite stays put where it was thrown.

But Hiram wouldn't part with it for worlds,
given to him, way back, by his uncle Vince,
he put in years in sail, and then signed on
the *Marie Celeste*, hasn't been seen since.

Vince had a sailor's gaze, he seemed to look
through and past you. He was momma's brother.
Taught Hiram a lot. That the length of a rope
was always only from one end to the other.

Taught him to leave rope cheesed or flaked or coiled,
never ever to let a loose end dangle,
the Devil grabs it; taught him how one man's knot
was always liable to be another's tangle;

taught Hiram to splice, tie a figure-eight,
bowline, clove hitch, reef, wall, crown, sheet bend;
taught him, only a green landlubber figures
that he can tell a beginning from an end.

Once, when momma was out, Vince showed him,
swore him in blood-secret, the lovers' knot;
the one no mortal can tie or untie ever.
But Hiram was only a kid then, and he forgot.

Entropy

Hiram and Jenny passed a sunny afternoon
together on the seashore, hunkered down
like little children, making them sand castles,
which grew into a pretty good-sized town.

Main Street, complete with churches and a courthouse,
schools and storefronts, fire-hall, a hotel,
boulevards all lined with dried kelp elms,
crowds of pebble-people; just as well

the whole thing couldn't somehow come to life;
most common folk don't ever really plan
on inhabiting infinities, or houses shaped
much like an upside-down tomato can.

And it was finished when they said it was,
and not before or after. We begin
at our beginnings, which are never-ending.
They sat back happy, watched the tide come in.

Not, nothing notwithstanding, they could stop it.
Moon being so determined to restore
to man, the lunatic who knows what crumbles,
the ordinary order of before.

Well

Pump skreeks like a bluejay.
Needs new leathers.
Has to be primed, Hiram
keeps a tin dipper handy.

Drinks creek water, mostly,
but sometimes in spring spate
gets roiled up, count on the well.

Hiram's daddy dug her,
before Hiram was born,
proper, cement collars
sunk about twenty feet.
Cool down there, summers,
keep a jug on a cord,
comes up real chilled.

Hiram's momma told him,
never you wish on her,
you might get it.

Call down her, softly,
she always answers
some hollow other name.

Look down her, sometimes,
the sun hung just right
overhead, see your own face
dim-shined, a stranger
encountered, or see maybe
the dark root of water.

Toxophily

Hiram made a bow in manual training
years back, he's still got it.
Osage orange and yew, bonded,
with a fibre backstrip. Neat.
Pulls forty-five pounds, near enough,
at thirty-one inches, which is
Hiram's draw to his chin.

Made his own bowstrings, those days;
number six Irish linen cord,
tacky with resin and beeswax, mixed.
Eye-splice at one end, timber hitch
at the other. Centre six inches
served with black linen thread.

Arrows the problem; always is.
Port Orford cedar, slightly tapered,
beautiful straight grain, smells
like Phoenicia must have, old days.
Fletched them with goose pinions,
Dancy brought in a great bundle
from his old man's Greylags,
tipped them with empty casings
from 32 cartridges. Chief Rae
donated a whole shoe-box full,
from target practice, he said.
But no two arrows, hand-made,
is ever exactly alike, flies
dissimilar. Like folks.

Trouble is, nowadays
how can Hiram use her?
Was never a hunter, Hiram.

Shoot up, might hit the moon,
pop her, let out all the air.
No call for collapsed moons.

Shoot down, a body might pierce
to the very heart of things.
Now that is real dangerous.

Shoot forwards, arrow can't go
nowhere, nohow; old Zeno, he
proved that, proper fashion.

Shoot backwards, a body might hit
himself as he was before,
and then where would he be
now? Too risky, by half.

But times, Hiram takes her down,
strings her up, plucks her
once or twice, ever so gently,
hears in the bass twang banjo
joyous O joyous!

Storm

Black boiling, low overhead.

Hiram hurries along the path behind the shack,
something he doesn't do that often,
having been drenched to the skin before now,
and having been struck by constant lightning
often enough in the past, left stone deaf
by massive continual thunder;

but this time, Silk's flat pasture is canted,
boulders scattered like shook pebbles
and Hiram casts several staggered shadows
at once in the close blue light and he sees
in a gap roiled back fast by black fists
a school of small stars veer in terror
and where is Jenny!

Art

Professor Alessandro Fausto Montefiore
put in for the job, only one, got hired
to paint up the Palace interior, years back.
God knows where he come from, some say
from Toronto, others Winnipeg, nobody
ever heard of him, tell you the truth.

Short, dark, chubby, nudging maybe fifty,
lots of curly black hair in fringes,
bald on the top, plump little hands,
talked a blue streak, never sat still
for a instant, eyes sad, like two prunes
in buttermilk. But smile like a child,
total. The women sure went for him.

Which is how come to this day Ma Tuggle
loafs in the buff above the proscenium.
Artemis, the Prof said she was, however
everybody hereabouts knows different.
No two faces like that, in God's Creation.

Thing is, one breast showing a nipple,
peeps right out of a gauze cardigan
sort of thrown over her shoulders.
Old Tuggle was fit to be tied. Besides,
there was her big rosy bum. Anyway,
somehow he squared it, give him credit.

Surrounding Ma Tuggle, a whole bunch
of bare-naked little boys, wrestling,
they were called Putti. And all kinds
of scrolls, vines, urns and bashed
columns, fancy. Two big oval faces,

one each side: on the right, laughing
fit to bust, is Comedy; one on the left,
scowling savage as old man Dancy
early Sunday morning, depicts Tragedy,
the Prof told Tuggle, keep him happy.

Also, a pink scallop-shell fountain,
small gold dolphins spewing out water
every-which-way onto a young lady,
also bare, but nobody quite sure who,
long blonde hair, might have been Mina Dancy,
only she's real snaggle-tooth, and prim,
over the main exit, back by the popcorn.
Got them their money's worth that time.

What he did, he painted the whole ceiling
a deep blue-black, with hundreds of stars
splattered about her, all shapes and sizes.
Must have used some kind of luminous
silvery paint; between short subjects,
the place blacked out, they glimmer
up there, faintly. Also several moons,
they being a kind of deep blood-orange.

Worked weeks at it, from a scaffold,
only hardly came down for his lunch,
crouched there singing away to himself,
from Grand Opera, softly, in Italian.
Didn't spill hardly a drop on the seats,
they were worried about that no end,
well, they were new, matched the carpet.

Then one night, he said he was done,
collected his money and took off,
owing Liz Dancy three weeks board,
last anybody saw hide nor hair of him.

Hiram asked Jenny, had she noticed,
things moving around up there, somehow,
one thin crescent moon, for certain,
used to be low down by the left exit,
now damn near dead centre ceiling,
and all kinds of constellations
come together and parted, real slow,
might take years; resembled beasts,
maybe, or Heroes, or strange Gods
to minds that wise inclined.

Jenny said yes she had, but cautioned
Hiram not to go on about it, folks,
they mostly don't care to know.
Got enough on their plate as it is,
what with crops and the Liberal Party.

Profile

Mooching around in Conlan's gravel pit, Hiram
sometimes found
fossils strewn about like ordinary objects
on the ground.

In sandstone shale, body apt to come across
anything,
leaves and fishes, trilobites, once a small
bird-like wing,

and once, intact, a woman's bitter countenance
that so spoke
to Hiram he was heart-pierced and he dropped it
and it broke.

Sometimes

Sometimes, at dusk, Hiram catches himself
dark in the tall mirror, his momma's glass
hung on the back of the door. Depending,
Hiram may give him a sort of a smile.
Sometimes he smiles back, sometimes not.
Depending.

'As cold waters ...'

Near as Hiram can figure it,
waiting his turn Saturday morning
in Alfresco's Tonsorial Parlour,
leafing through yesterday's Clarion,
World Events Section, inside back page,
next to the Maritimes Bowling Notes,
we got us about as much chance, just,
as a celluloid cat being chased
by a asbestos dog through downtown Hell,
as Hiram's daddy would put it.

Fact: we got us The Bomb, clever,
blow us to smithereens ten times over.
Fact: we got us a bunch of bomb-happy,
ostrich politicians in power. All nations.
All talking about Defense, sidewise,
and saith, Am not I in sport?
Just a matter of time. Of which
we got plenty, and not much left.

As a dog returneth to his vomit.
But Hiram been around long enough
to have a healthy respect for cats.
It's not that they got them nine lives,
only one life hereabouts, we all in her,
but ninety-and-nine ways, maybe more,
of being alive, which is different.
Furthermore, Hell was never next door,
no more than is ever Heaven. Durable.
Consider; Market Report. In the Courts.
Social Notes. Weather. The Sports Section.
Companions Wanted. The Comics. The Stamp
Corner. Marriages. Lonelyhearts. Births
and Deaths. Your Garden. The Good News.

Slide Show

Hiram escorted Jenny to a slide show
and Strawberry Supper, which was put on
in the United Church basement assembly,
in aid of the Organ Restoration Fund,
the pump organ being missing several
fairly important pipes, according
to young Bob Dodson, who played her
most Sundays, and kept on threatening
to go back to the old wheezy harmonium,
now resting out in the drive shed.

It was Scenes from Around the World.
Ladies Aid to provide the supper,
with no set price, supposed to pay
according to conscience, which meant
a nickel from Tuggle, he having invented
the widower's mite, so Hiram figured.
Pretty full house, though, considering;
word got around, some of the scenes
featured ladies from Bali and suchlike.

Jimson, who caretakes, had rigged up
a sheet on a quilting frame, hung
it in front of the Bible Lands map.
Worked pretty well, when it stopped
wobbling. Lot of the slides cracked,
having travelled themselves, by now,
across most of the Maritimes, come
from the W.M.S. head office, Toronto.

Minister said a few words; Brotherhood,
Fellowship, thanks to the Good Ladies.
The sad state of the organ, but how
The Lord provides for His own. Applause.
Then Jimson put out the lights, was giggles
from couples sitting towards the back,
plugged in the lantern, took three cords,
and cranked her up. Smoked pretty bad
at first, till the dirt burned off,
but then settled down. Like always,
just about every other one backwards,
or upside down, or both. Causing Jimson
who right away burned his hand, to say
a few words inappropriate in His House.
But nobody bothered, all part of the show.

The Taj Mahal, by moonlight, first off.
Arches, all scribbled with Arab script,
shimmering marble domes. And no organ.
Then off to the Scottish Glens. Damp.
Some highland cattle, they minded Jenny
of Zack Danson, before he was put away.
Terraces in Nepal, zigzagged on sheer slopes,
must have pretty good legs, grew rice
and crescent patches of flowering mustard,
with white mountains piercing clouds
and keeping on going up, for background.
Then cities of Old China, with thin boys
pulling on rickshaws, or maybe was men,
all of them wearing the same wiped faces.
Eskimos sitting on hundred acres of ice
by a seal's air hole, dark harpoons ready,
backs straight, legs stretched straight out
like fur dolls set at a kid's tea-party.

Mixed bunch of scruffy Indians, east, not red,
clutching a tiger, dead, like a striped stain
poured over the fierce bright jungle scene,
grinning, triumphant, proud for themselves,
one with his head in her propped-open jaws.

Well, might have known, comes the big moment,
was Balinese ladies, but all very modest,
seen from behind, while watching the sunset
blaze boats with their menfolk returning;
and African ladies, they wore Mother Hubbards
of saffron and purple and emerald green,
and startling smiles, all toting bibles,
of course, and numerous fat happy babies.

Afterwards, Jenny having a numb bottom
from the wood slats in the folding chairs,
and in need of massage, they bypassed
the Strawberry Supper. And besides which,
United Church is emphatic on Temperance,
while travel gets to be real thirsty work.

Hiram figured, no point making mention,
not even to Jenny, of what he had seen,
seemed, in one white flash between slides:
a figure transfixed, an agonized face,
disturbing familiar, it wasn't his momma,
gone deathly with love and entreaty.

Street Lamp

Under the crimped green galvanized-metal reflector,
numberless frantic insects home to the one weak light
that hollows a small pocket into the huge darkness,
the fragrant moonless surrounding summer's night:

some are the churning, split-back beating beetles,
impossible in the air, with ridiculous little wings,
some are elaborate tinsel ephemeral structures
unfolded; light and other unfathomed desire brings

this haze of motes, midges, a smoke of iota lives
that flutter, plunge, gyrate, that skirt around
and around, casting a swift, exaggerated shadow
below, criss-crossing the insect-littered ground.

Hiram, sauntering, languorous, late from Jenny's,
watches a vast battering death's-head moth
singe, and seared, like a tawny velveted pebble
drop, for death is cut from the one whole cloth.

Jenny's Ears

Jenny's ears are sizeable, flat,
small-lobed, pointy, set high,
right one slightly more-so,
delicate spiral-coiled,
pierced by her grand-momma,
flushes up when kissed.

Left one pretty deaf, since clobbered
by Bill, her husband, long way back.

Nevertheless, she hears lots
that most folks don't, rightly.

Storms on the way, maybe tomorrow.
Children thinking to cry.
Small fear-sounds in long grass.
Music appointed, sometimes.
The long waves about to break, and broken.
Night birds in passage, way up, faint.
Cats washing rhythmic in sunlight.
Some shades of green-blue. As in plums.
Anyone laughing proper.
Twitched nostrils of mares, when she passes.
Their moist standing breathing.
A crystalline ring, brittle, of some stars.
Hiram's heart not beat.

Blood

Sheep are peculiar. Jenny
raised an abandoned lamb.
Tenderness and a bottle.
Grew up to be a ram.

Horns curled like Truth.
One night, Jenny asleep,
deathly, her Ram took up
the blood-burden of Sheep.

Butted the wounded moon
after the absent sun.
Butted every pierced star
to darkness one by one.

His yellow unblinking eyes
burn now by Jenny's side:
keep until First Morning
watch over His Bride.

Jenny's Radio

Jenny has a radio,
a pointed walnut box.
Knobs and scroll-work on the front.
Inside, yowls and squawks;

takes a while, to warm her up.
Behind the cardboard back,
little flimsy yellow lights,
can see them through the crack.

Get you Big Band Dancing,
from the Ritz Hotel
roof garden, on cold winter nights
comes in clear as a bell.

Can get you Inner Sanctum,
someone should oil the door,
Green Hornet and The Shadow,
Tony the Troubadour;

also, Amos and Andy,
Baby Snooks, Fibber McGee
and Molly, Information Please,
The Craigs, on C.B.C.,

Quiz Kids, Lum and Abner,
Cheerio, Treasure Trail,
Jack Benny, Charlie McCarthy,
Fred Allen without fail.

And Jenny likes to listen,
sometimes, to the soaps:
One Man's Family, Helen Trent,
Big Sister, how she copes.

Hiram cautions Jenny,
says it isn't wise,
listen too much, consider
Granny Kline's demise;

Granny, fiddling with the dial,
heard a great voice declare
'Repent ye, for the end is nigh!'
and took to the air.

Offer

Hot summer days, Hiram loafs about Karen's wharf.
Tide comes in, considers, after a while goes out,
steady; a tangle of various masts' wavering shadows
grows short, then gets longer again. That's it, about.

Real peaceful, which Hiram savours. But once a seal
plopped up his head, his whiskers dripping, and said,
'Well Hiram!' Hiram nodded, cautious; the seal belched,
fishy, continued: 'Say, Hiram, things is dead,

deepwise, nowadays. Poseidon, he packed it in,
some time ago. Claimed, it was too much stress;
pollution; the subs; Amphitrite, she wearing him down;
don't rightly know if you'd noticed?' Hiram said, 'Yes.'

'So, Hiram,' seal said, casual, 'we were thinking that you
might care to take over the job, bring your banjo?
We got us a need.' Hiram shuddered, knowing the cold's
bone-stealth, the crushed lightless abysm. Said, 'No!'

Memorial

Down at the Cenotaph, a pair of green field guns.
Kids sit in the tractor-seats and turn the cranks.
Town Council put them there, with the help of the Legion.
Tuggle suggested a couple of beat-up tanks.

Cenotaph lists the names of Our Valorous Fallen,
two World Wars. Hiram's daddy was mustard-gassed,
just a little, at Vimy, 9th April of seventeen;
then they asked, would he go to Russia, but he passed.

Wheels set in cement, so jokers can't move them;
Schultz welded most moving parts; no firing pin;
can't lay or train them. Was wood plugs in the muzzles,
but kids pulled them out to put firecrackers in.

The Unknown Soldier, at ease, with his Ross rifle
butt upwards, his head bowed, in bronze, life-size.
Hiram once saw him look up and nod to his daddy,
they passing alone together and caught his eyes.

Hiram figured it out, you could fire the left one,
Would hit St. Ewald's smack in the ogive door,
fire the other, would knock off the Baptist steeple.
Everything fair, like they say, in Love and War.

Error

Hiram's discovered desire is to enter water
as light enters water and alters it not,
yet sets quick fire beneath the surface,
as rapture may enter a body held in thought;

even as water remains the reflecting semblance
that turns burning, that casts back shattered fire
manyfold into the blinded beholder's eye,
to enter water discovered is Hiram's desire;

even as cold motionless depths unsounded
by light or the lost rumour of light remain
haven of absent creatures, beings we deem
monstrous for light stricken from their domain;

yet into this radiant world Hiram and Jenny
slip together, bright in each other's sight,
as a vessel, surging, divides the featureless waters
that cleft, curled, breaking, may enter light.

Autumn in Eden

Frost on the long grass, mornings. Ella-Sue
finished her green-tomato relish. Grailey Bates
put on the storms himself, with Porson gone
to live with some hippie lady in the States.

A few left on the trees, but they are scabbed;
most of the possible apples are on the ground,
rotting. Wasps have found them. The deer will.
Chronos is slowing down. But he gets around.

And around, and around again. Which just might be
His deep undoing. The other day Hiram saw
fat Mary naked, bathing, near blue with cold,
grab for her towel. Sure. But it sticks in the craw.

Not Yet Death

The sun is shrunk in Hiram's eye
beheld, a pinprick fire
encompassed and encompassing.
Given unto desire,

the folds of darkness kindle
with beasts, released, that sweep
flame before them, skeltering.
Hiram is asleep.

Hiram's Burden

Milkweed these days clustered
with Monarch butterflies;
Well, hardly credit it,
save for my own eyes,

one of the orange creatures
wavered, flamed, grew tall,
turned, standing before me,
into Apostle Paul.

Short, stocky, balding,
grey bird-nest beard,
got a sword, a book of words;
said, 'Don't be afeard,

Hiram, where butterflies
cluster, Apostles is.
Just a simple matter
of metamorphosis;

which is mostly a matter
of how folks care to see;
getting to be a lost art
just between you and me;

mainly, milkweed's milkweed,
butterfly's butterfly.
Can't blame them, kind of
difficult otherwise;

but just wanted to tell you,
things is coming along
much as they was and will be.
But Hiram, don't get me wrong,

got to keep being Hiram
striving, for all your worth;
else nobody won't inherit,
won't be no blessed earth.

Means, keep pickin' banjo,
off and on, night and day;
keep hankering, but hang loose.
Nothing much more to say.

Anyway, folks don't listen,
most of them too uptight.
Well, better be going;
got me letters to write.'

Next thing, was just milkweed,
and me hanging about.
So ambled on to Jenny's.
But sadly, she was out.

Conceit

Jenny saw a cartoon in the Clarion,
title was, *Inside the Sun*.
Pictured a fat geezer, in his undershirt,
feet propped up on a crate, reading
a crumpled copy of the Sun Tribune,
in need of a shave, battered slippers,
smoking a cigarette. Well, he's got
a bunch of electric fans rigged up
on a mess of extension cords; there's this
huge riveted machine over to one side,
with a lever set at R I S E. Outside
his window, inferno.

And saw Hiram, *Inside the Moon*; huge,
in Grailey's old buffalo robe, ear-muffs,
gauntlets, the purple and orange toque
and scarf she knit him for last Christmas,
five-buckle galoshes, shivered all over;
the lever of his machine set, of course,
to F U L L, or maybe W A X; he busied
like Charlie Chaplin, drilling holes
with a brace-and-bit in a wedge of green
cheese. No heaters about, and no window,
just a big photo of Jenny in a bikini
pinned to the wall. Proven to be better
than wood-stoves, winters.

Banjo

Things to the contrary,
Hiram keeps fooling about.
Late nights, maybe, or slow
summer afternoons, tranquil.
Times, if a body is dead
lucky, banjo takes over,
Hiram is what's what.
Not often, natural, but
more than enough. Hiram
thereafter goes forth
respectful and disrespectful,
sobered and joyous. Once
only, Hiram was near why.
Wasn't, of course, else
might not have got back
with his skin. Still,
a close thing, somehow,
to nowhere, particular.
Body has to be grateful,
if cautious a while, while
things settles to things,
attended. Deo gratias.

Ice House

Staunch Calvinist, though man may err,
Gaunt digs down for what is there.
Under sawdust, that's full of fleas,
lies last winter's two-foot freeze
from Tuggle's pond, near thirty tons,
chock-a-block, kept from the sun's
transmogrifying habit. Gaunt,
who's got more hid than man can want,
scrabbles, grunts and heaves, to hump
a hundred pounds out to the pump
and wash her off. Although two wrongs
don't make a right, with Hiram's tongs;
since Hiram borrowed, years ago,
Gaunt's best crowbar. Quid pro quo.
Gaunt keeps discrimination nice;
for fair is fair, as ice is ice.
But Hiram figures he'll manage fine:
his having turned long since to wine.

Event

He called Hiram by name. Hiram.
But didn't say His. Hiram
given to understand, He each
has numerous, all depending.

So Hiram asked first Angel,
would He care for a cup of coffee,
there was some left in the pot;
but He declined, polite.

Second Angel never turned round.
Stood looking out at the night,
which was moonless, clouded, black.
But His back view resplendent;
being all various molten eyes.

Third Angel, Hiram told him
He looked a bit like Lana Turner,
in the movies. He seemed pleased.

Fourth Angel tried for a while,
teach Hiram to juggle a apple
and two small balls of fire.
But Hiram couldn't quite get
the hang of it, somehow; singed
him one sideburn and quit.

Asked fifth Angel about the Unicorn
Hiram thought he spotted in Silk's
garden, early morning, last week,
eating young lettuce. Angel said,
was unlikely, but you never know.

Hiram requested of sixth Angel,
would He mind not Glorying
quite so much; neighbours,
Gaunt in particular, might think
the shack was on fire, call out
the Brigade. Angel complied.

Not that He had much small-talk
among Him, to speak of; could be
heavy going for some, likes to gossip,
but suited Hiram, content to adore.
Not any old night, after all.

Then was one of those moments
of silence, sudden; He all
looked up together, expectant:
seems, seventh Angel was passing
over. But He didn't Assume.

So after a while, He trooped back
into the candleflame. The wicker
rocker scorched a bit, on the seat,
where Hiram was sitting, the shack
scented, slightly, like beeswax.

Left Hiram feeling a bit let down,
natural. Is difficult, body don't
quite get the message. Another time.
Maybe. But was close.

Time

Hiram's uncle Dubois Carleton,
forty-four years on the railroad
back in the good old days
when the six-fifteen pulled out
at six-fifteen, or the world
would come to an end, right then
and there. Was forced to retire,
he reached the age. Still active,
big man, but sorrowful somewhat,
since Annabelle passed on.

Sometimes, at table, would bend
a fork over his railroad watch,
rattle off message in morse, fast,
that would make young Halton
choke on his mash, and blush
up fierce. Intrigued Hiram.

Used to show Hiram the watch,
watch it go round together. Dub
said it had more real jewels
than Ma Tuggle; said, the third
hand was the second hand; said,
want to see her go backwards,
just turn her face over. Said,
won bets with that one, often.
Was hot-boxes, wires gone down,
sleetstorms, derailments, wars,
just kept going round and round
on its own accord. Told Hiram,
don't ever lose track of accord.

Well then, there was Red Calhoun,
dowser. Famous for not washing.
Didn't want to be shut up with Cal
in a close room in winter. Dowsed
with a fresh hazel fork, most times,
though a bent coat-hanger would do;
but stubborn ones, would dangle
his watch, a battered old turnip,
on the end of its silver chain,
having taken the elk's teeth off.
Worked. Hiram was witness, often.
Always found sweet water. Plenty.

After he got back, Leonard
laid his issue wrist watch
on the anvil, pulverized it.
Still starts crying, silent,
sometimes, for no reason
but not so much anymore.
Folks pretty good, pretend
they don't notice.

Hiram hasn't a timepiece.
Is Jenny's, she left it one morning
way back, it's in the top drawer
of the dresser, but neither
ever remember to wind her.
But share a mortal respect,
recollecting, both, for accord.
More and more, time goes by.

Gleeman

Hiram acquainted with grief,
and has met despair;
doesn't entertain them much,
but they are there.

Got to know Gaunt's first wife,
Ellen, before she died,
left him with seven sickly kids;
Gaunt was fit to be tied,

she took off that abrupt.
She told Hiram, because
tired of trying to make bricks
out of Gaunt's last straws.

Not much Hiram could say,
right then, or not to her;
he sitting in for Bones,
Mister Interlocutor,

hearty, all ready to pose
first question, just as soon
as previous top-billed turn,
Gilda The Deadpan Moon

with Roses The Slapstick Sun,
finish the comic relief.
But Hiram already met despair,
not unacquainted with grief.

At First Sight

Was years back, at the Fall Fair,
Jenny consulted Madame Sirena,
Seeress; Your Future Revealed!!!
Which required crossing her palm
with silver; a dollar in fact.
It getting on afternoon, she
being badly in need of a drink,
was slightly snappish with Jenny.
Told her, she had Blood and Love
in her past, but would soon meet
tall dark and handsome stranger;
then hustled her out of the tent,
slapped C L O S E D sign on the fly,
leaving Jenny somewhat annoyed;
could have done better, cheaper,
with her niece Cleo and tea-leaves.
Trouble is, Cleo goes, sometimes,
on into her fits, starts moaning
truths you don't care to hear.

Was just about then that Hiram,
having invested a dollar cash
at the Rotary Lucky Dip, pulls out
Rotary stickpin with one small
glass diamond, and fortune cookie;
message inside, rolled up tight
said, 'Support Rotarians!', also,
about to meet up with a lady,
will be short, blonde and lovely.
Hiram not exactly enthralled;

but the dollar supposed to go
for the Old Folks' Retirement Home,
so passed on the stickpin to Feely,
who prized it, and fed the cookie
to sparrows, who didn't much.

Well later, Jenny was standing
in the Palace of Mirrors tent,
sees short, grotesquely swollen
Stranger with squashed pin head
and retractable feet beside her,
puckered-up, lamprey mouth.

Hiram observes her in turn,
squeezed thinner than Olive Oyl,
sky-high, split down the middle,
head comes to a sharp point,
beaked, fingers a foot long;
a Harpy in person, smirking.

But both beholden to brightness
abounding within and beyond
distortion, appearance, reflection,
they burst out laughing together,
at themselves and each other;

not really stopped since. Later,
agreed it was Fate, of a sort.

Possible Improbable

One night, on the yellow oilcloth.
Hiram had shuffled, reshuffled,
and Jenny had double-cut.
Going to have a friendly game
of beggar-my-neighbour, or snap.

Jenny got up, to put on the kettle
and Hiram for no good reason
turned the deck over and fanned
out the cards. There she was!

Deck had gone back, entire,
to original order; each suit
running from ace through to king,
suits in their proper sequence,
spades to clubs, with the joker
sitting, alert, on the bottom!

Jenny stared, and went deathly.
Hiram fell mortal silent.

Was an old souvenir pack
from The Intercolonial Railway
and Prince Edward Island Railway,
the route of the 'Ocean Limited'
(During the Tourist Season)
and the famous 'Maritime Express'
(The Year Round). Backs featured
a moose sporting a huge rack
poking out of a port-hole-like
red seal, said 'People's Railway'.

Faces had oval Maritime scenes:
'The Bore, Petiticodiac River',
'Some New Brunswick Beauties'
(salmon, not ladies), 'Yachting,
Sydney Harbor', 'Steamer *Scotia*,
crossing the Straits of Canseau',
'Morrissey Rock, near Campbellton'
'Home from the Hunt, New Brunswick'
(featuring very dead moose),
'Pabineau Falls, Bathurst', 'Ruins
of Fort Louisbourg', 'Mulgrave',
'Bull Cart, Matapedia', 'Reversing
Falls, Running Up, St. John', same
running down. Was Dub's deck, once.

Anyone tell you, it can happen;
and everyone tell you, it won't.
Hiram and Jenny the only two souls
in the whole universe, know for sure
that it did. Once. At least.

No point in phoning The Clarion;
anyway, Hiram not on the Bell.
No point, writing to Mr. Ripley;
would be Not, for absolute sure.
No point, framing the deck somehow
for posterity. Posterity just snicker.
Seems the point was, was no point.

So after a while, shuffled them up,
went back to normal. But Hiram,
left somewhat restless, began
out of habit slowly constructing
a card house; collapsed, jumbled,
attempting to build second level.

Weeks later, Hiram discovered,
the Joker gone missing; Jenny
confessed, she had taken it,
chucked it into the woodstove.

Couldn't say why, to Hiram.
Asps and Camelopards. Dolmens.
Palisades. Helms. Berserker's
cornflower eyes. Fire. Fire!

The Pogey

Jenny received a card
from a computer. Said, 'Sir:
you have been selected at random.'
Signature a blur.

Hiram likewise. His read,
'Madam: may this find
you as well as it finds me.'
Was unsigned.

Gaunt got one; 'Darling,
weather *divine!* Miss you.
Should see the topless beaches
here! X X X Etaoin Shrdlu.'

Tuggle's read, 'Ms. Togule:
this card has been sent
to you in error. Hi,
I'm Ed Broadbent.'

Feely baffled by his;
'Parameters still to be
defined, Resurrective
situation. Hopefully, J.C.'

Well, seems the Unemployment
Insurance computerized,
at vast public expense.
Hiram not surprised.

'A *lump bred up* ...'

What goes on in Porson's head
is no sooner done than said.

Boy's a fool, at sixty-nine.
Got his mother's mouth, not mine.

More I hang around, the more
grasp I get of what's in store.

Taciturn. Well, better be,
going on for ninety-three.

I got the Word. And the less
said the better. Boy's a mess,

and his lady's just as bad.
Or maybe worse. Sure was glad,

when they lit out for the States;
just the place for Porson Bates.

Got me some quietude at last.
Trouble is, too good to last.

Judge Clayton

Agnostic, Cynic, Rationalist,
he is a good man, and just;
ironical; humorous; kind;
one prepared to be judged,
who rejoiceth not in iniquity.

And would give anything
(as he might be aware)
to be given anything other
than what is the given: save
that which he cannot give,
since it is not, evidently,
at his disposal; assent.

But from his frequent dreams,
whether he tumbles with wet women,
rude and loudsome and joyous,
or walks strait through the door
left ajar into the severed light,
to look down upon living water,
or turns, slowly, tears streaming,
to greet and enfold her again,
or at last grasps the austere
elegant mortal distinction,
lethal, or keeps effortless
pace with the rare fleeting
of like pierced creatures
over terrible greensward,

he holds remnant delight
awhile, Human, and cries,

silently, wakened, 'O'.

Brightness

Uncanny, sometimes, tricks
the spring light can play;
Hiram and Jenny each saw,
one pale Groundhog Day,

the other's standing shadow
banished where they bled,
severed, out from underfoot:
went back to bed.

Moth

Jenny doesn't care for moths:
once heard one declaim;
'Mortal Jenny! Look on me!
Cindered in your flame!'

'I bear eyes that cannot see!
Scales that cannot fall!
I am Beginning! I am End!
I am All in All!'

Well, maybe so: but Jenny
long wary of the dark;
endless metamorphosis;
the exclamation mark.

Whiteout

As the snowstorm raged
absolute everywhere,
Jenny beat over to Hiram's ...
But he wasn't there.

More than God would number;
no two, they say, the same.
Hiram was on his way to Jenny's
and nobody to blame

if each missed the other
struggling, head bowed down,
gale-blinded, half-way into
and half-way out of town;

chance sees man abandoned.
God, we are told, lacks
of nothing. Surely mercy
covers Our tracks.

Inundation

1   Basement the profound abyss.
Attic bright with spume.
Corpses, surfaced, jostle
in the living room.

Upstairs in the bedroom,
upon the seamless swell
Hiram rocks, immersed in dream,
briefly bound to dwell

in this Immortal edifice,
inhabited to keep
Gods, long jealous of the dead,
instant in his sleep.

2   Jenny wept. And Hiram
couldn't say why.
Is the burden of this world,
makes one cry:

envy, beauty, calumny,
sorrow, fear, relief,
solitude, rage, jealousy,
intolerable grief.

Death is irretrievable.
Passion may redress
absolute Atlantis,
founder Lyonesse.

Classic

Doing his Bogart bit, Hiram
pulled down his slouch fedora,
lit a Lucky Strike with his Zippo,
turned up his trench-coat collar,
shouldered his way into Jenny's;

'Okay, shweetheart, now lishen ...'
stopped dead in his tracks.

Wasn't Jenny, but Ms. Medusa,
sitting playing three-handed bridge
with Ms. Stheno and Ms. Euryale
at Jenny's card table. They all
puffing at menthol cork-tips,
sipping iced stingers, also
a plate of moly fudge to hand.

For a moment, was only a low
susurration of serpents.

'Just what we wanted, a dummy!'
commented Ms. Stheno, sidling
up from her chair, lethal-graceful.

'Come to get stoned, Big Guy?'
crooned Ms. Medusa, inviting,
patting her upsweep, careful.

Ms. Euryale said nothing, shuffled
the deck as if she had done it
for ever and ever. Smiled.

'Polydectes sent me ...' said Hiram
thinking fast, stalling for time;
went for his shoulder-mirror,
but having problems, what with
all of the trench-coat buttons,
cross-tabs, flies and whatnot
being done up tight for effect.

The ladies squealed, and dived
for cover, remembering Myth;
but not much space under one card
table, besides, had a wonky leg
which Hiram been meaning to fix,
collapsed on top of them, dumped
playing cards every-which-way,
serpents furious, carpet a mess,
what with spat venom, squashed fudge,
smouldering butts, spilled drinks.

So Hiram got out fast, smart,
Hero outnumbered; also, snakes
give him the willies. Beat it
back to the shack, had a couple
of stiff drinks. Decided, which
he already knows, that more,
in common with most ladies,
to Jenny than meets the eye.
Is still hopeful. Oh yes.
But got to brush up, obvious, on
Perseus act, and practise
his fast draw. Would be wise,
before playing Hero again.

Role

Ephraim Silk's eldest, Sheldon, was found drowned,
face down in the town watering trough: big affair,
cast iron, green, with curlycues, the I.O.D.E.
had it installed back in 1910, is still there,

in front of the Courthouse steps. Not used much now,
except by tall dogs and kids. Hiram's aunt Ruby said,
leave a horse hair, will turn into a living snake;
however Sheldon got in her, he's most certainly dead.

Sheldon a looker and knew it, he never could pass
a mirror without glancing; carried a barber's comb
in his back pocket, used orange-blossom brilliantine.
Ephraim said, he was just busting to leave home,

get into the movies. Dead certain he'd be a star,
what with his profile, he worked steady on his smile,
went to Miss Hartshorne's, evenings, for elocution,
even took tap, by correspondence, for a while.

Truth is, that nobody hereabouts much mourns him.
Was a death by misadventure, Judge Clayton ruled.
When Mina Dancy, later, as much as declared him to be
the putative father, Belle Hartshorne, for one, not fooled.

Countenance

Hiram for years now been nursing a mortal notion.
Fact is, as Jenny knows, notion enfolding him.
Some days, almost, can tell you just how it goes:
but once you begin with telling, it's sink or swim.

Seems sometimes, mornings, elusive as last light;
sometimes, evenings, seems like too much to bear,
ever; sometimes assumes the Alpha and Omega;
worst is, sometimes, it seems as if nothing there.

Hiram tried once talking it over with Feely;
thing is with Feely, got to take her real slow,
which is about right for suchlike considerations;
but Feely just shook his head, picked banjo.

Also, has tried confiding somewhat to Jenny.
But discerned, somehow Jenny already knew
more than she might let on; well, mortal matters,
he should have reckoned, persons like Jenny do.

Figured maybe he picked it up from his momma;
wherever she got it, seems she had it by heart,
the whole kit and caboodle, simple, as always.
His daddy, he might have had it too, for his part.

Meantime, leave it be, way some things taking
their own good time; yet seems a body may just
come to remember, earth to incorruptible earth,
ashes to kindled ashes, dust to enamoured dust.

Great Blue Heron

Feely, at home in the marsh,
watched as the bird stopped
being a limb of driftwood
thrust up out of the reeds,
unfolded and flapped, heavily,
neck crooked, beak levelled,
legs trailing, a short bit
to another pool; more frogs,
crayfish, pollywogs even,
or possibly small perch.

Stalked, in deliberate slow
motion; froze; glared
baleful about and down
at the amber shallows, set
to transfix quick lives.

And minded Feely again,
of the other rapacious
and sometime foreseen
formidable bird, the one
that after arduous flight
settles at last, aflame
and unscathed, come
to impregnate the sun.

Gladson

A wizened little old bugger, but
Ned Gladson as tough as they come.
In his seventies now, can still read
the fine print on the Castoria label
without glasses. Got all his own teeth.
Can pee six feet; when Silk, wistful,
asked him how come, said, 'Massage.'

The boys are all big, and real hellers,
but for Morley, who got himself saved;
Chief Rae, he would nip round the block,
Saturday nights, to miss closing time
at The Dominion House and the Gladsons,
taking their leave, rumbustious, somewhat.
But if Ned says 'Jump!' they jumps,
double quick, backwards or sidewise.

Could still haul lobster pots all day,
if he chose, which he don't, no more.
Sits on his porch, mornings, make sure
that the sun comes up. Naps, most noons.
Then back on the porch, bolt upright,
see that she sets proper. Important,
somebody got to, he says, or else.
And nobody going to argue, not with Ned;
Besides which, he may be right; who knows?

Offered, one warm night, to arm wrestle
the Prophet Isaiah; two out of three.
But the Prophet backed down, saying,
'... the whole head is sick, and the whole
heart faint.' Gladson just spat, got on
with the job, waxing the cuticle moon.

Comic

Feely went on backstage at Thimble Theatre,
try to get Popeye's autograph. Had to settle
for Roughhouse's; seems Popeye can't write.
Roughhouse's surprising, real elegant chancery,
swash R, with elaborate paraph depending, much
like Elizabeth One. Well, got to remember, cooks
is deceivers ever. Wimpy been called, often,
a son of a seacook; but was most hospitable,
he offered, kindly, to loan out to Feely
his rubber suit, for the forthcoming United
Church Turkey and Wild Strawberry Supper.
Popeye can cipher some, but not read. Seems
he shipped out, age eight, boy seaman before
the mast. Learned seamanship, proper, but not
what you'd call schooling. So Olive seconded,
is Popeye's amanuensis. Handles his mail,
reads him the Maritime News from The Clarion,
evenings, is planning to co-author, for Faber,
his autobiography; *Some Seas I Have Sailed.*
Popeye offered, teach Feely, free of charge,
his Crouch-me-duck-stoop punch; would be useful,
encounter neckless bruisers, but Feely declined,
never could scrap, too late to start now.
Besides, sudden, a cold dank gloom settling
down over everything, Feely figures correctly
The Sea Hag at hand; and Feely don't care,
meet up with her. Not again. First time,
draped over a bollard like a wet black net,
was enough. Was not what she said, Feely
already worked most of that out for himself,
or the ebb-muck stench, but her voice; her voice,
and the black light back of her good eye.

Violence

Also, Belle Hartshorne played harpsichord.
Scarlatti, the Bachs, Rameau,
Couperin, were her passions.
One night she was playing a slow,

intricate fugue, probing,
Sheldon came in with a sledge,
smashed it to pearwood smithereens.
Belle went right over the edge:

they made love on the rug, sobbing.
Then Sheldon lit out. For good.
Belle left the mess lie there untouched
for weeks. But she understood.

Commission

Feely could do him three things
good as anyone, better than most;
could pick banjo, could whittle,
could just be. Last is not easy.

Well, anyone can, after a fashion,
whittle, like most of the menfolk
did, sitting around complaining:
whistles, ships' hulls for kids,
maybe a decoy snipe. But Feely,
he had the knack. Pastor Gwyllym
said, he could carve, proper.

And greatly admired a set of seven
interlocked rings, delicate work,
Feely cut out of the ash loom
of the oar that big Morley broke
at the Baptist Dunk and Regatta,
when he didn't feather proper;
never did know his own strength.
Pastor asked him, would he attempt
a Crucifixion some time, for over
the altar at St. Ewalds. Had one,
from Church Furnishings, Boston,
Limited, but nothing to brag on.
Feely said that he'd ponder it,
left it at that. Wasn't too sure,
about Gwyllym. But Moira, his Mrs.,
always been kind with Feely, some
wasn't, give him a hard time.

So after a while, picked him up
a big block of seasoned hemlock
from Tuggle's yard. Nobody looking;
but figured, wasn't much wanted.
Hemlock's a bugger to work, grain
is bewitched, contrary, always apt
to run any however, mess you about.
Set her up at the back of the byre,
nobody going to know save Feely,
the cows don't care, and commenced.

Beavered away for weeks, nights.
One hundred watt bulb, bare, hung
from the rafters, was not too bright,
but sometimes the shadows helped.
after a while, seemed Feely got
mortal involved in the undertaking,
didn't get over to Hiram's for ages,
neglected banjo, got real broody.
Not that anyone noticed, folks
accustomed to not notice Feely.

Also, uncommon, he always being a slow
but sure whittler, somehow he nicked
him his right thumb, deep, got blood
all over the figure, despite himself.
But didn't seem to impede any. So,
at last, one night, real late, Feely
finished her off. Done. Best he could
manage. Had him a lot of trouble,
getting the countenance just right,
but seemed like he had help. Maybe.
Feely too pooped to know. Left her,
greatly relieved, she was finished.

Next morning, went back to look, see
maybe she needed a last touch, also
give her a first coat, linseed oil.
Cross there, perfect, if bloodstained,
but vacant. Somebody swiped Christ
Crucified: leastwise, no longer present.
Well, Feely pissed off! But recovered;
dismantled the cross, hid her away,
abandoned the whole thing. And never
mentioned, not even to Hiram. Still,
was sorry, let down Mrs. Gwyllym. She
never could comprehend, natural.

Hiram's Dread

What was not yet
apparent set
fire to the sky.

And folks ran out
of doors, about
like ants, to die.

Some cursed, some wept.
And Jenny slept.
And darkness came.

For Jenny bore
awakened, more
than mortal flame.

Conger

Hiram was in swimming, eel
eeled up, give him the eye,
said, 'Eel you ain't, Hiram.
Not even a passable try.

You out of your element, baby;
now, don't mean to be rude,
but man immersed lacking real
eel verisimilitude.

Granted, not everything halcyon,
out in your Sargasso sea;
breeding and feeding never was
what it's cracked up to be,

but better than being human.
Been thinking about it a lot
ever since elverhood; any eel
can tie herself in a knot,

emulate God's meander: but,
eels can also untie again.
Humans, they just not up to it,
got too much on the brain.

Don't care to be disrespectful
of anything that squirms,
but eels figure the human brain
is one mortal can of worms!

Leaves you, both land and water,
a tangled hell of a mess.
We eels feels real sorry
for humans, I must confess.'

Hiram regarded him, thoughtful;
but having nothing to hand
to thump him with, wallowed,
dog-paddled back to land.

Phone Call

After the troublesome dream, Hiram
somewhat concerned for his Aunt Ruby.
So rolled him eleven rolls of pennies
from the marmalade jar on the dresser
and cashed them in for some silver;
went down to Pountney's Drugs, tried
to phone to Vancouver, British Columbia,
speak with his cousin Japhet, resides there.

And first try lucky, in comes Japhet,
clear as a Bell. Says, 'Hiram, your Aunt
Ruby doing okay. She got herself hooked
on Holistic Healing, Aura-ology, the whole
Alternative Life-Style. Traipses about
in designer jeans, size fifty-six, Peace
sweatshirt, Cowichan headband, don't wear socks,
ever. Moved on out to the Gulf Islands;
grows top-quality grass. She commutes
to Nanaimo couple of times a month, runs
her a Consciousness-raising group, for cash.
Well, was during one of which, she claims,
she ascended even unto the Right Hand
of God; or was maybe the Left, she not sure
which. But man, she is cleaning up. Not
to worry, Hiram, Ruby with it in spades.'

So Hiram rang off, and had enough left
for a root beer float, couldn't explain
why he felt saddened, remembering her
frail as a cornstalk husk, often elsewhere
in the same room, silent for nights at a time,
her eyes honed inwards, alert, with her thin
elaborate hands clasped in her dress-lap
like motionless answers, or her head bent,
her hair fallen forwards, fragrant, enclosing,
speaking the dreamwords low over his crib
on long, light-shimmered evenings, summers.

Changes

For firstly Jenny became a body of water,
voracity and again and again moon-heaved,
constant with other identical music.

Then Jenny became a body of fallow land
grazed by the sweet-breathed multiple beasts,
stricken flint-quick to sharp fires.

Later, bodyless light, was everywhere
entered and entering, calyx-illumined
in darkness beyond our abounding.

Become various thus with the least creature
lost, just. And fire the simple fire unceasing being
embodied. Who knows now. At last! At last!

Tempest

Wasn't a soul, remembered ever seeing it that bad before.
Hiram huddled aft of the mainmast, scared out of his wits.
Leviathan spewed:

Lost Scriptures. Patched rubber waders. Prophets, forgotten. Orts.
Snapped masts and entangled rigging. Harlots in dishabille. Three
dud petards. Various Regency fops. Landladies, massive. One mauve
Squid. Bottles in ships. A thirty-year run of The Bangalore Times.
Couples attempting exotic coitus, without much success, on swings.
Ambergris. Puncheons of ardent spirits, unbroached. Plato's ideal
collar-stud. Two portly butlers and various pale catamites, weeping.
Josephine's reticule. Absalom's vade mecum, with some pages blank.
A Dervish, stilled. The tackle box that fell off the punt's transom.
A pot of Hermione's quince pickle-conserve. Oodles of condoms.
Washing, still pegged to the line. Nine-tined forks lacking handles.
Old Braggadocio, gaping in disbelief. Oxyrhynchus papyri in terrible
disrepair. Latchkeys beyond all numbering. The glazed skull of a pigmy
shrew in perpetual snarl. Lot's nuptial sheets once vainly displayed.
Pennants, faded and frayed. Griswold Lorillard's tuxedo, in, alas,
mothballs. Axolotls becoming axolotls. A very small knothole, said
to have come from the True Cross. Suicide notes, holograph, signed
and unsigned. Twin cities in aspic. A Cambridge wrangler. Bicuspids
of failed Saints. A luna moth pinned flat. Her hazelnut, carved
in the likeness of Yahweh. The bottle of Ketchup that couldn't be
opened. The Angelic Doctor's Swiss Army knife, with a tool for
removing corns. A posy of pink mignonette, tied with sweet rafia.
Syd. A warlock's dried Roger, complete with wart. Howdahs littered
with junk mail. Most of the spectrum. But not all. A pop-up folly,
with eremite. A jam-jar of Archimedes' rancid bathwater. Jack
Armstrong, the All-American Boy, disgruntled. Two aspirins and

bed-rest. A dun. The middle conundrum. Gladstone's spats. Slime mould on the move, and about to spore. What she said, afterwards. Lord Kelvin's patent log registering nought. Circe's botanical sketches, in pastels and water-colour. Burke's bedside lamp. Frass, bio-degradable. Six tumbrels of green dung, ditto. Fanny's first, tearstained, dance card. Dildos, officers, for the use of, Mark VI. A tin-type of Gaurisankar in summer. A shoe thrown by Bucephalus. And much, much more, friends.

But Ms. Leviathan soon gobbled it all up again.

'Shoe Clerk Says, Come Back Again
and We Fit You With The Box The Shoes Come In'

Hiram knows this loopy lady, Adelle, lives in Quebec,
she is into reincarnation these days. Real heavy.
Casts horoscopes on the side, makes her a bundle.
Runs what she calls a Dream-Boutique, in Levi.

Learned to curse in patois-French from her old man,
singe your ears. He was a runt habitant lumberjack,
he went out on the spring run back in sixty-eight;
all she knows for sure is, he hasn't come back.

Gets out a mimeograph Newsletter, sends it on to Hiram;
she calls it, *Adelle's Report from the Other Side.*
Last issue all chit-chat with Consuela, a recent friend,
she being a seventeenth-century Portuguese child bride.

Things was rough, back in those days, for young ladies,
spent most of the time, apparently, down on your knees,
scrubbing or praying. Now, Consuela didn't speak French,
never mind English. And Adelle never learned Portuguese.

Well, live and let live. Hiram's momma mostly would sing
hymns while she redded up. '... His bright Crown adorning'
one of her favourites. She died peaceful, just about dusk.
Told Hiram, you reborn, remembering, every morning.

Interview

Things being slow, no good fires or murders,
cub reporter, Dale, from The Clarion, sent
out to interview Hiram on the occasion of
his first two-hundredth birthday shindig.
Starters, Hiram showed him the telegram come
from the Queen; read, 'Go for it, Hiram!',
more or less. He was greatly unimpressed.
Likewise, with the Gideon Bible borrowed
by Gaunt from the Lord Nelson Hotel, it had
all of Our Savior's actual spoken words
underlined in red ink by a findings drummer
and some querulous marginalia that Hiram
figured must have been penciled in by Edward
Bouverie Pusey, first-class Tractarian gloss.
A munificent birthday gift! However, Dale
not into the Bible, never encountered Gaunt.
Then Hiram offered a corner slab off the cake,
which he took. But bit down hard on a dime,
near broke an incisor, was most unhappy.
So gave Dale some root beer, had some himself,
fierce laced with pusser neaters, a gift
from Earl Rae, confiscated. Got cheered up,
and began by asking Hiram, of course, to what
did he attribute.... etc. Hiram said Banjo.
But Dale didn't get it, so Hiram switched,
cackled something dumb about clean living
and clean thinking, been practising at
his codger's cackle, got it down pretty good.

Then Dale asked him, what was the most
important event in his whole life. Said,
Life. Dale thought he repeating the question.
But let it go, and asked Hiram did he have
any advice for the young? Hiram said no.
What the Hell, no point, considering Dale,
to try rementioning Banjo, waste of time.
Asked Hiram next, but cautious, just how come
he had never served in the Armed Forces
all those years, all those world wars? Well.
Hiram inspired, threw him a slow curve, said
he had to admit, to tell you the honest truth,
at recruitment, had always lied on his age.
So inquired, who was the most unforgettable
character.... just like the Reader's Digest.
But Hiram could hardly name the Unnameable.
And who could cipher Feely to likes of Dale?
So pretended to nod off sudden. Is useful.
Besides, Jenny was listening, also getting
somewhat impatient, she does, waiting for Hiram
come to bed and Rejoice in the Celebration
amongst them Again and Always. Anyway, Dale
figured he had enough, keep the Editor happy,
so tip-toed out of the shack, shut the door
careful, drove back into town, thinking on how
to soft-pedal the last Town Council Meeting.

Problem

Tea was not a total success, on account
of Hiram getting himself stuck again;
this time, on the low-piered foot-bridge,
in the shallow Blue Willow saucer.
Jenny hung in, and made conversation
as best she could do, but it flagged.
Three purposive travellers, watching
the sunrise, they said, had passed over
and left him transfixed where he gazed
into the riverheart of reflected light.
Above, the combustible parakeets blazed
blue. No going back, the cannon-ball tree
did not permit it. And yearning, as Hiram
had long since learned, will not suffice:
to enter the summer-house one must become
one with the ultimate blue motif and flow
farther than Hiram, still too aware of
denial, of the various staggered fences,
their formal declared grammar of inner
and outer, of blue bounds of blueness,
is able. One does not readily violate
blue abundance, and who among us is ever
prepared for the white-glazed abeyance,
how shall we know intricate gold figured
about the brim? For we are beholden. And,
had it not been for the pair of drunks
in their bent reed punt, happy with rice
whisky and seven fat carp still gasping,

who hailed Hiram and offered him vulgar
hilarious passage to nowhere particular
out of the perfect circles it seemed
he might have remained rooted to blue
until forever the gnarled, flamboyant-
fronded egregious willow was felled.
But they did, as it happened. And Hiram
had him a nap, after the company left.

Crux

No. And yet, and yet.
Hiram is willing to bet
(though he's not a betting man)
that bright barn swallow can
with no trouble at all
fly through the solid wall
of the barn and out again.
Which goes against the grain;
miraculous, so to speak.
She got bugs in her beak,
is fast as a gnat's blink.
Well, must be an unseen chink,
allows of it, somewhere.
Mostly, Hiram don't care
to pass judgement on things.
with or without wings.
Folks don't pay no heed
to The Venerable Bede
hereabouts much any more,
and Hiram don't set store
on the likelihood they will.
Most things is dodgy. Still,
Bede, he was nobody's fool.
As somebody remarked, a rule
there to be proved, as best
a body can. Consummatum est.

Hosts

Well, Handel Shadwell having driven into town,
to purchase a batch of Coogan's day-old bread
and a haunch of somewhat whiffy sealworm cod,
Cherry figures she better get out the lead.

Got six couples due to arrive on Friday night;
four of them Mr. & Mrs. Smith. So who cares?
Doesn't pay these days, inquire of marriage lines;
point is to charge whatever the traffic bears.

Set on the back of the stove what the locals call
Shadwell's Jesus soup; because He could walk
on it, the story goes. Cherry couldn't care less
what the locals say, always was busybody talk.

Most of the sheets, not all, can be just turned,
after they're aired a bit. Saves on the soap,
Smiths not fussy, got other things on their minds,
hotter nor pepper-sprouts. Well, a body lives in hope.

Bananas and jello do for dessert, bananas is cheap;
reduced to sell, in fact, you take them turning black.
Handel says, with a dollop of luck, the septic tank
should hold out over the long weekend, not blow back.

Is not all beer and skittles, not by a long shot,
taking in trippers. Never know what you might get;
like that lady snake-charmer, into chains and leather,
revealed, she was a man, sort of. Tuggle not over it yet.

Handel should never have told him, but he gets mouthy
after a few, they being loyal Brothers, up at the Lodge;
still, Tuggle helped out over the Paki Fire-Inspector,
and put Handel on the claiming Gran as a tax-dodge.

However, home is where the heart is. Regular, winters,
Shadwells take off for Florida, book into a trailer camp
in the Everglades, gets a bit buggy, but is not expensive,
and neither Handel or Cherry overly bothered by damp.

Hiram knew Cherry, was Cherry Dancy then, in Grade School.
Showed everything to Ted Tuggle, back of the bike shed,
so Ted claimed. Swapped comic books with Anse, and later on
they started going steady. Caused talk. But Anse is dead.

Tutelary Spirit

Jenny feeling definitely broody, goes for a long amble along
the shore. Comes across a stranded, standard service issue,
barnacle-encrusted Bombay Gin bottle, seemingly fully empty.
Considers a bit, then, what the Hell, she pulls out the cork.

Whoosh! Out comes Lord Baden-Powell, in a great pink cloud,
reeking of juniper. Was him for sure, know him anywhere, even
despite of his slightly askew jade-green turban with pigeon's-
blood ruby, the flowing daffodil blouse and the coral slippers
with curled up toes, because of the blue serge shorts, the belt
with the clasp knife and pea-whistle. Salutes, three-fingered,
lefty, sneaks a quick look at his compass, adjusts his lanyard.

And bows slightly, says, 'My dear young lady, how extremely kind.
Deeply indebted. Most salutary, sea air, after a long confinement.
Now. Your three wishes. At your service, Ma'am.' Looks expectant.

So Jenny tells him, she hasn't three wishes, but only just one.
He nods acquiescence, conceals his impatience, waits politely.
So she requests. Lord Baden-Powell blanches, aghast, staggers
a pace backwards, recovers, blurts, 'Impossible! Madam, think
of the Dear Queen! And Albert's disapprobation would utterly beggar
description! My Dear, I'm afraid not. Sorry. It's just not on.'

Jenny reminds him, coldly, of Scout's honour, not to mention
Cub's. Suggests, he could try shutting his eyes and think on
the Empire, if that made it any better. Says, she expects more
of a Peer's promise, a Gentleman's word. However, is bounders
abounding, these days, even in high office. Is a great pity.

Well, Baden-Powell, he rocks back and forth on his heels, chews
at his lip, mutters a few latin tags to himself, turns puce.
Then, suddenly, smiles, draws himself up, regains his composure.
Says, 'Yes. Well. A chap's word is his bond. It shall be done.
However, my Dear, since you didn't specify *when....* Your wish
shall be granted: yet, as Scripture reminds us, to everything
there is a season. A time, doubtless, to sow, to reap, and even
to do as you have requested, may come, Deus non volens. Quite.
Until then, Madam, your servant.' Pouff! He disappears within
another great blast of gin fumes, takes with him the bottle.

So Jenny turns back and heads for Hiram's, somewhat cheered up,
thinking herself on the Empire, with, however, her eyes opened.

Golden Jenny

Having got himself a new vice, old Doc Herman
is somewhat abstracted, during afternoon surgery
and evening house-calls. Not that Tuggle's piles,
however fractious, were ever a source of endless
fascination, save to Tuggle; and when you see
one dose of galloping clap, you've seen them all.
Praise be, for penicillin. And Juliette Coogan's
confinement looks to be awkward, much as usual;
he expects to be called out of his bed, later.
Juliette always being one for the small hours.
He is not looking forward to having to tell Belle
Hartshorne, what she already knows, that it is
indeed cancer. Female plumbing, well, male too,
for that matter, being a profound, not inelegant
basis for the longstanding argument over Proof
from Design. Doc Herman is not sure, even
after all these years, which way he might side.
Delivered so many babies, he has long lost count,
and never once heard any Angels singing; still,
Doc thinks that speaks more of himself, all things
considered, than of Angels. And who knows, maybe
tonight's the night; they did once, so it seems,
and who is he to say, that they have ever stopped.
Well, any country G.P. is privy to more secrets
than the entire Curia; but of the earth earthy.
You name it, Doc Herman has seen it before.
Meanwhile, there is his brand new vice; tonight
he may tie the unique, delicate, absurd wonder
he has so vividly dreamed; with gold-eyed hackle
wings, crimson silk body, jet horsehair antennae,
an impossible creation no self-respecting trout
would look at twice. And name it in secret homage
after her: lovely beyond compare, improbably lethal.

Accident

Hiram fell.
No real damage done, but
sure flusters a body.
Picked himself up (no
mean feat, that), dusted
himself off, discovered
that he had tripped over
Archimedes' one fixed point.
Not all that big, when you get
down to it, but stubborn.

So figured, why not, and cast
about for a lever of sorts.
Only thing to hand, just
might serve the purpose,
too flaccid by far; well,
Hiram getting on, natural.

But just about then, Jenny
came in, tousled, towelling
her hair, after her bath,
roseflushed and fragrant and
softly sayd: deare hart, how
like you this?

Anyway, to make a short
story long, as that macho
son-of-a-bitch put it,
the earth moved.
Therwithall.

Hiram Heretical

Now in the beginning was the Word, remember, brother!
Well, say someone jostled God's elbow, simply accidental,
would be difficult, to pinpoint exactly who's to blame,
causing Her to dribble some of Her primordial hot soup
all down the front of Her best Sunday bib-and-tucker.
Well, say She started to cuss like a trans-Canada trucker
and into the dangerous world there leapt at one fell swoop
the first Hiram, blushing, astounded, but nevertheless game.
Which, as Creation Myths go, seemed to Hiram pretty elemental
and, he told Bible Bill, is just about as good as any other.

Bible Bill, however, turned pink in the chops, fit to be tied,
got himself red hot under his dime-store celluloid dog collar.
Called Hiram by every name in the book, kindest being blasphemer,
demonstrated considerable creativity. Which was not surprising;
Bill, he was William then, his mother insisted, back in school
had him an early oily turn of phrase. Was keen on the Golden Rule,
for others, clean living and thinking, prayers and early rising,
Bible study, keeping himself real pure in the eye of the Redeemer.
Nowadays, Hiram has to admire, he makes him a pretty good dollar
pulpit-thumping, Fundamental, and colonic irrigation on the side.

Marriage

Judge Clayton having a little trouble with his latch-key,
returning to his chambers, very late, from participating
at the silver wedding anniversary, down at Art's Delicafe,
rented out for the occasion, of the Irresistible Force
and the Immovable Object. Feeling no pain, so to speak.

He having officiated, they both being, back in those days,
agnostics, at their wedding. Which was, he remembers, quite
an affair. Not the Ceremony, it was civil, short and sweet;
they both bridled a bit at 'obey', of course, but went well
otherwise. The Reception after, however, was something else.
Poseidon having been Bridesmaid, and Hecate the Best Man,
the speeches were memorable. The Groom, as well, outdid
himself; said, in reply to the toast from Bride's father,
'Pops, think not that you are losing a daughter, but rather
that you are gaining a dependent.' Which went down well.
Poseidon, he gave the happy couple his latest invention,
a horse; and Hecate, not wishing to be outdone, proffered
various dogs, honey and black lambs, of which she had lots.
All of which caused something of a sensation at Wasaga Beach,
Lake Huron, where they honeymooned for a fortnight, blissful.

Well. Lots of water under the bridge since. The Judge suspects,
somebody, Loki maybe, spiked the domestic Labrador Champagne.
Everybody looking older and greyer, even Chronos, who either
dyes his hair, or else is sporting a top-quality rug nowadays.
Best thing was, swarms of little children, all shapes and sizes;
their union having proved fruitful beyond anyone's expectation.
Were plenty, in fact, who said it could never last. Just before
he fell asleep in his swivel chair, his crook stogie having left
yet another scar on the rolltop desk, the Judge remembered how
he heard, he thought, a voice declare with a terrible clarity
even as they turned to embrace, 'All Human Forms identified ...'.

Hero

Morley Gladson hit a homer.
Bottom of the ninth, with nobody on;
soon as he connected, he just knew
that ball was gone.

Was a two-all tie, with two out,
a three and two inside sucker pitch,
changeup, and Morley really slammed
the son-of-a-bitch!

Flounders defending the County title,
being last year's Lobster League champs;
The Clarion said, they'd be real lucky,
beat the War Amps.

Needless to say, all hell broke loose.
Morley sauntered across the plate,
having walked, grinning, round the bases.
Which was just great,

save for one small thing; seems somehow,
all eyes upon it, centre field, the ball
diminished, vanished. Thing goes up,
she got to fall,

natural; not this time. She took off
right on out into the noonday sun,
didn't come back. Well, Art Bouchard
can't call this one,

Umpire's Book of Rules don't cover
ball goes into orbit, that much plain;
so he called the game, day being bone-dry,
on account of rain.

Well, after the fracas, one of the best
anybody hereabouts remembers ever,
Morley said, must be the Lord's work.
Maybe. Jenny never

told a soul, but just as Morley swung
she happened to catch his daddy, Ned,
making a hex sign. Awkward, he now being
two years dead.

Piscators

Plato turned up unexpected, so he and Hiram went fishing.
The weather was ideal, but they went anyway regardless.
Hiram forked over the compost heap, filled a beans can
with earthworms, having no gentles or hellegramites to hand,
while Plato considered things, as he did mostly a lot of.
Borrowed Silk's skiff, and Plato bailed while Hiram oared.
Had them a good afternoon, what with Plato having provided
a goatskin of vintage retsina, and Jenny not having made
a stack of bolony and pickle sandwiches that didn't exist.

Plato outlined his plan, open a greasy spoon, specialise
in shish-ka-bobs and Greek salad, trendy, would call her
Food For Thought Cafe, his wife's family put up the money,
they being anxious to diversify. Bus boys no real problem,
Thrasymachus, Glaucon and Adeimantus keen to be waiters,
Plato would be the brains of the operation, trouble was
finding a good short-order cook. Socrates considering it.
Hiram allowed as how it might catch on, but cautioned him,
folks hereabouts not much on essential forms, prefer steak.
But then there is always the trippers, might go for it big,
never can tell, city life alters the palate. Plato agreed.

Speaking of trippers, Hiram asked after the late Fulton H.
Anderson; Plato admitted as how he was holding his end up,
but did tend to run on somewhat. Hiram remarked, the road
of excess leads to the palace of wisdom. And also, as how
eternity is in love with the productions of time. Plato
looked up sharp at that one; not huffy, but didn't comment.
So Hiram let the subject drop, finished off the retsina.

Got back about sunset, Plato having to catch the last car.
Hiram figures, Plato the most accomplished damn fisherman
he has met in a dog's age; put Jesus Christ on his mettle.
Doesn't actually ever *catch* anything, of course. But good.

'The red plague rid you ...'

The washing was out on the line
overnight, and it froze
as stiff as old souls.
You don't think those
are the ice cream Emperor's
absent underclothes:

Hiram's turkey longjohns,
as plain as your nose,
or Jenny's bikini briefs
in scandalous pose?
No. Well, probably not.
You might, had you chose,

have resorted to fact.
Had the question arose;
Life, as we soon learn,
permits of such gloze.
God may, you say, die.
But She don't doze.

Hiram on the Night Shore

Crashed slabs of blackness
advancing. Moon may come out.
Anything might. Blind violence
leaves room for doubt.

If it does, and is dolphin-borne,
which it's not as a rule,
Hiram will take up cap and bells
to play the fool

to his own kind in the vouchsafed,
thereby ensilvered night.
If it doesn't, he will remain
in motley, despite

the shingle's gripe, the great rage
wasted before his feet.
Only so far shall waves advance,
so far retreat.

Contents

Richard Outram was born in Canada in 1930. He is a graduate of The University of Toronto and lives in Toronto, where he works for The Canadian Broadcasting Corporation. He is the author of *Eight Poems* (1959), *Exsultate, Jubilate* (1966), *Turns* (1975), *The Promise of Light* (1979), *Selected Poems* (1984), *Man in Love* (1985).